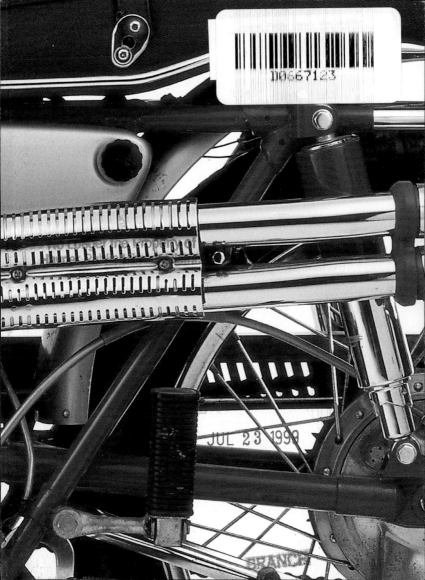

HONDA

CLASSIC MOTORCYCLES

HONDA

HUGO WILSON

DORLING KINDERSLEY

DK PUBLISHING, INC.

A DK PUBLISHING BOOK

PROJECT EDITOR PHIL HUNT
ART EDITOR MARK JOHNSON DAVIES

SENIOR EDITOR LOUISE CANDLISH
SENIOR ART EDITOR HEATHER MCCARRY
MANAGING EDITOR ANNA KRUGER
DEPUTY ART DIRECTOR TINA VAUGHAN
US EDITOR RAY ROGERS
PRODUCTION CONTROLLER ALISON JONES

First American edition, 1998

2 4 6 8 10 9 7 5 3 1

Published in the United States by DK Publishing, Inc.,
95 Madison Avenue, New York, New York 10016

Visit us on the World Wide Web at http://www.dk.com

Library of Congress Cataloging-in-Publication Data

Wilson, Hugo
    Honda / by Hugo Wilson. -- 1st American ed.
        p.   cm. -- (Classic motorcycles)
    ISBN 0-7894-3509-8
    1. Honda motorcycle--History.   I. Title   II. Series.
TL448.H6W55   1998
629.227'5--dc21   98-17159
                                                                      CIP

Reproduced by Colourscan, Singapore
Printed in Hong Kong

CONTENTS

INTRODUCTION

The Honda story was initially about
transportation. Once the company
managed to get postwar Japan mobile,
it looked for other challenges, such as
selling bikes in Western markets; by 1960,
Honda was the biggest motorcycle
manufacturer in the world. Another
challenge was to beat the greatest
names in motorcycle racing; Honda
won its first Grand Prix in 1961
and has kept on winning ever since.
In addition, Honda has continually
sought to prove its engineering
excellence and commitment
to sell motorcycles for every
conceivable market. Today
Honda is still the biggest in the
world and still the most successful
in every form of motorcycle sport.

HUGO WILSON

HONDA TIMELINE

HONDA'S EXTRAORDINARY COMMITMENT to provide a motorcycle to suit every conceivable market niche means that the variety of bikes it has produced in its 50-year history is remarkable. Everything from simple commuter scooters to awesome race bikes is available from the Honda catalog. Its dedication to the four-stroke engine wavered during the 1970s, and it now produces several two-stroke machines.

CB92 BENLY

THE EARLY DAYS

The first Honda machines had frames and forks made from pressed steel, with styling that was distinctly Japanese. Most early bikes had small-capacity engines, though they increased in size during the 1960s.

• 1950s   • 1960s   • 1970s

THE 1960s

By the time the awesome CB750 arrived in 1968, the frames were tubular and the forks telescopic, with the styling of the bikes now tailored to Western markets. The use of bright paint jobs and chrome typified the 1950s Hondas.

GOLDWING

THE 1970s

After the success of the CB750, Honda thought that the more sophisticated the bike, the better it would be. However, most customers disagreed, finding the Goldwing too big, complex, and heavy.

CB750

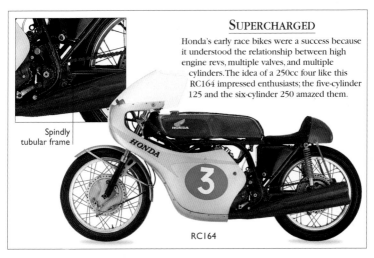

SUPERCHARGED

Honda's early race bikes were a success because it understood the relationship between high engine revs, multiple valves, and multiple cylinders. The idea of a 250cc four like this RC164 impressed enthusiasts; the five-cylinder 125 and the six-cylinder 250 amazed them.

Spindly tubular frame

RC164

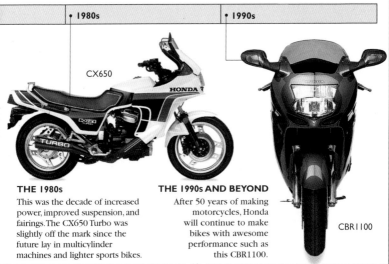

• 1980s

• 1990s

CX650

CBR1100

THE 1980s

This was the decade of increased power, improved suspension, and fairings. The CX650 Turbo was slightly off the mark since the future lay in multicylinder machines and lighter sports bikes.

THE 1990s AND BEYOND

After 50 years of making motorcycles, Honda will continue to make bikes with awesome performance such as this CBR1100.

1960 CB92 BENLY

• HONDA MAKES ITS MARK EARLY ON •

COMPARED TO THE EQUIVALENT 125cc machines being offered by
European manufacturers, the Benly was a revelation. It produced
15bhp at an unbelievable 10,500rpm, a striking contrast to a 125cc
BSA Bantam, which made less than 5bhp at 5,000rpm. Honda
specifications included large alloy drum brakes and electric starting,
but the impressive feature list came at a price, and the Benly was
as expensive as many larger machines. However, even they couldn't
match the Honda's specifications or, in many cases, its performance.

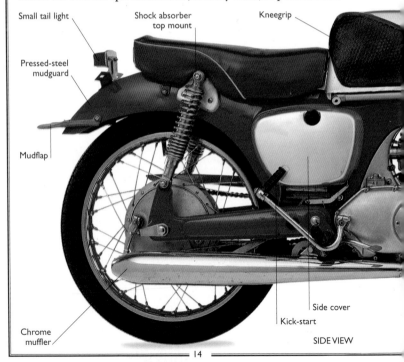

Small tail light

Shock absorber
top mount

Kneegrip

Pressed-steel
mudguard

Mudflap

Chrome
muffler

Kick-start

Side cover

SIDE VIEW

SPECIFICATIONS

- **ENGINE** Overhead camshaft, parallel twin
- **CAPACITY** 124cc
- **POWER OUTPUT** 15bhp @ 10,500rpm
- **TRANSMISSION** Four-speed, chain drive
- **WEIGHT** 220lb (100kg)
- **TOP SPEED** 70mph (113km/h)

Flyscreen

Speedometer set in headlight nacelle

6-volt headlight

THE HEAD OF HONDA

Soichiro Honda started his motorcycle business in 1948. From humble beginnings, Honda quickly became the largest manufacturer of motorcycles in the world.

Steel mudguard

Pressed-steel fork

Ribbed front tire

Single carburetor

Large-diameter drum brakes front and rear

Suspension linkage

1963 C100 SUPER CUB

• HONDA'S CLASSIC IS BORN •

THE HONDA SUPER CUB IS THE most successful motorcycle ever built. Since its introduction in 1958, over 21 million have been produced, and models based on the original are still in production in 11 countries. In 40 years the design has been upgraded, but the original concept remains the same. An overhead camshaft engine replaced the overhead-valve design in 1966, and variants with increased capacity were also produced, some with electric starters. The classic Super Cub remains an essential means of transportation in some countries of the world.

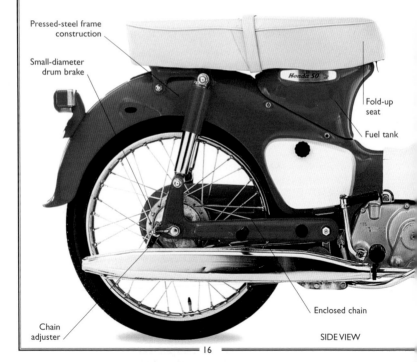

Pressed-steel frame construction

Small-diameter drum brake

Fold-up seat

Fuel tank

Enclosed chain

Chain adjuster

SIDE VIEW

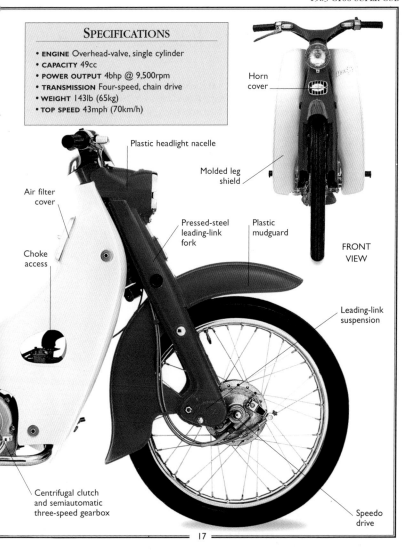

SPECIFICATIONS

- **ENGINE** Overhead-valve, single cylinder
- **CAPACITY** 49cc
- **POWER OUTPUT** 4bhp @ 9,500rpm
- **TRANSMISSION** Four-speed, chain drive
- **WEIGHT** 143lb (65kg)
- **TOP SPEED** 43mph (70km/h)

Horn cover

Plastic headlight nacelle

Molded leg shield

Air filter cover

Choke access

Pressed-steel leading-link fork

Plastic mudguard

FRONT VIEW

Leading-link suspension

Centrifugal clutch and semiautomatic three-speed gearbox

Speedo drive

1964 CL72

• HONDA DELIVERS A MORE CASUAL BIKE •

EARLY HONDAS PERFORMED well but, to Western eyes, looked a little odd. Honda realized this and quickly replaced the pressed-steel construction and angular look of the early bikes with modern tubular frames and more conventional styling. With the CL range, Honda borrowed styling ideas from off-road machines to produce good-looking, fun bikes. This CL72 is a typical example.

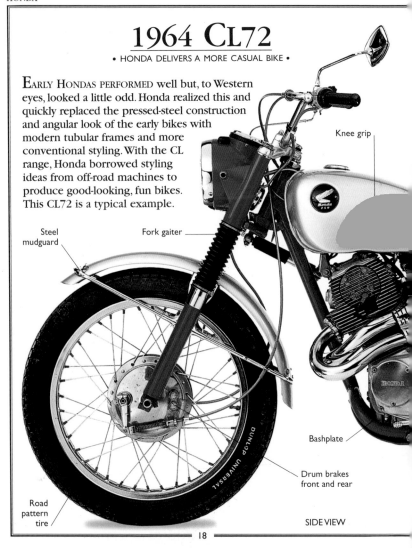

Knee grip

Steel
mudguard

Fork gaiter

Bashplate

Drum brakes
front and rear

Road
pattern
tire

SIDE VIEW

18

HIGH-PROFILE ADVERTISING

Honda changed the image of motorcycling in
the 1960s with advertising campaigns showing
happy young people having fun on their Hondas.

SPECIFICATIONS

- **ENGINE** Overhead camshaft,
  parallel twin-cylinder
- **CAPACITY** 249cc
- **POWER OUTPUT** 24bhp
  @ 9,000rpm
- **TRANSMISSION** Four-speed,
  chain drive
- **WEIGHT** 337lb (153kg)
- **TOP SPEED** 80mph
  (128km/h)

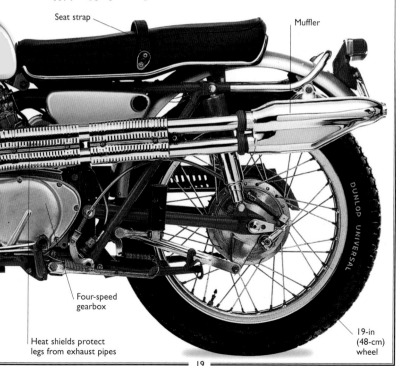

Seat strap

Muffler

Four-speed
gearbox

Heat shields protect
legs from exhaust pipes

19-in
(48-cm)
wheel

DUNLOP UNIVERSAL

1964 RC164

• HONDA'S EARLY RACE BIKE OUT TO PROVE A POINT •

Honda soon recognized that if it were to convince the world of the superiority of its four-stroke bikes, it needed to achieve success on the racetrack. In the early 1960s, the company spared no expense or effort in its quest for Grand Prix victories. This 1964 250 was the final development of Honda's four-cylinder 250 racer. It was unable to match the performance of the Yamaha two-stroke and was replaced the following year by the incredible six-cylinder machine that took the World Championship back to Honda.

Rev counter

Ribbed front tire

Alloy wheel rim

Telescopic fork

Green background signifies 250 class

Large-diameter drum brake

SIDE VIEW

SPECIFICATIONS

- **ENGINE** 16-valve, double overhead camshaft, in-line, four-cylinder
- **CAPACITY** 249cc
- **POWER OUTPUT** 45bhp @ 14,000rpm
- **TRANSMISSION** Six-speed
- **WEIGHT** 232lb (105kg)
- **TOP SPEED** 140mph (225km/h)

HONDA'S RACING 250S

Tom Phillis was one of several riders to race the 250cc four-cylinder Honda between 1960 and 1964. Here, he sweeps to victory in the 1961 French Grand Prix.

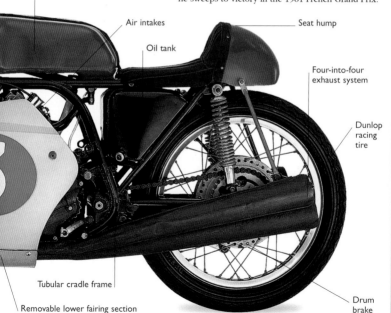

Fuel tank retaining strap

Air intakes

Oil tank

Seat hump

Four-into-four exhaust system

Dunlop racing tire

Tubular cradle frame

Removable lower fairing section

Drum brake

1969 CB750

• THE FLASHY FOUR-CYLINDER SENSATION •

HONDA'S NEW 750 CAUSED A SENSATION when it was launched in 1968.
It was fast, flashy, and, above all, it had four cylinders – advertised by
the four separate exhaust pipes. No other manufacturer offered this
level of performance, reliability, or features. The combination of five-
speed gearbox, electric starting, and a front disc brake was not
offered on any other large-capacity machine. After its release, no
rival manufacturer could afford to ignore it.

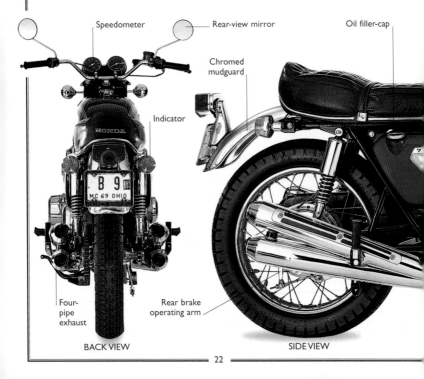

Speedometer

Rear-view mirror

Oil filler-cap

Chromed
mudguard

Indicator

HONDA

B 9
MC 69 OHIO

Four-
pipe
exhaust

Rear brake
operating arm

BACK VIEW

SIDE VIEW

HONDA BADGE

The CB750 was Honda's first attempt at the prestigious 750 market. The bike continued with updates until the late 1970s, when Honda introduced an all-new CB750 with a double overhead camshaft.

SPECIFICATIONS

- **ENGINE** Overhead camshaft, four-cylinder
- **CAPACITY** 736cc
- **POWER OUTPUT** 67bhp @ 8,000rpm
- **TRANSMISSION** Five-speed, chain drive
- **WEIGHT** 485lb (220kg)
- **TOP SPEED** 124mph (200km/h)

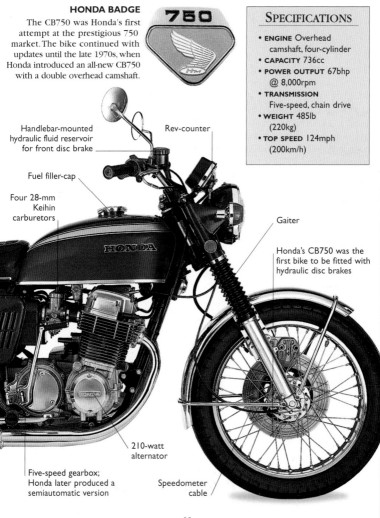

Handlebar-mounted hydraulic fluid reservoir for front disc brake

Rev-counter

Fuel filler-cap

Four 28-mm Keihin carburetors

Gaiter

Honda's CB750 was the first bike to be fitted with hydraulic disc brakes

210-watt alternator

Five-speed gearbox; Honda later produced a semiautomatic version

Speedometer cable

1975 GL1000 GOLDWING

• FROM SUPERBIKE TO TOURING BIKE •

FOLLOWING THE SUCCESS OF THE CB750, Honda lost its lead in the superbike stakes to Kawasaki's four-cylinder 903cc Z1. In an attempt to reestablish its position, Honda introduced the 999cc Goldwing in 1975. It was certainly bigger, heavier, and more complex than the Z1, but it was not universally acclaimed – handling was suspect and performance wasn't particularly impressive. Detractors even suggested that Honda had built a comfortable, but bland, two-wheeled car. However, when touring enthusiasts began fitting the bike with fairings, panniers, and other accessories, the bike found its niche as a superb long-distance machine.

Grab rail

Seat strap

Dummy fuel tank;
real one is under seat

GOLDWING
GL1000

Muffler

Rocker cover

Shaft final
drive

SIDE VIEW

SPECIFICATIONS

- **ENGINE** Overhead camshaft, horizontally opposed, flat-four
- **CAPACITY** 999cc
- **POWER OUTPUT** 80bhp @ 7,500rpm
- **TRANSMISSION** Five-speed, shaft drive
- **WEIGHT** 571lb (259kg)
- **TOP SPEED** 120mph (193km/h)

Dummy tank houses electrics

High, wide handlebars

Side reflector

OVERHEAD VIEW

Brake hose

Chrome mudguard

Radiator

Camshaft drive cover

Twin front disc brakes

1976 CB350F

• THE ORIGINAL SUPERBIKE'S BABY BROTHER •

AFTER PRODUCING THE best-selling 750 four, Honda went on to make smaller versions of the groundbreaking design. A 500cc four was introduced in 1971 and an even smaller 350 in 1972. Both shared many features, though no components, with their larger-capacity stablemate. While the 500 achieved considerable popularity, the good looks and impressive performance of the 350 failed to catch on. It was redesigned in 1974 and capacity was increased to 408cc, creating the CB400F, which went on to become one of Honda's best-loved models.

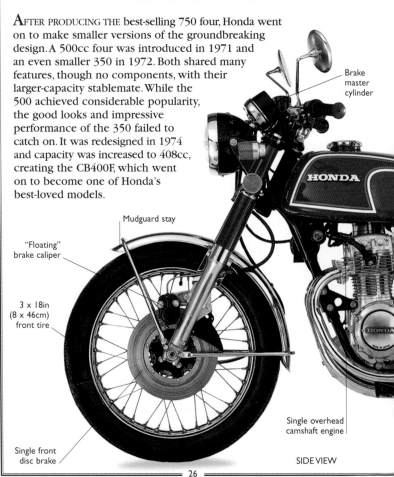

Brake master cylinder

Mudguard stay

"Floating" brake caliper

3 x 18in (8 x 46cm) front tire

Single front disc brake

Single overhead camshaft engine

SIDE VIEW

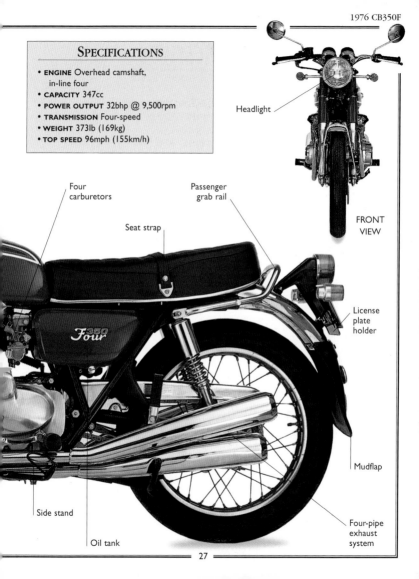

SPECIFICATIONS

- **ENGINE** Overhead camshaft, in-line four
- **CAPACITY** 347cc
- **POWER OUTPUT** 32bhp @ 9,500rpm
- **TRANSMISSION** Four-speed
- **WEIGHT** 373lb (169kg)
- **TOP SPEED** 96mph (155km/h)

Headlight

FRONT VIEW

Four carburetors

Passenger grab rail

Seat strap

License plate holder

Four 350

Mudflap

Side stand

Oil tank

Four-pipe exhaust system

1980 CR250 ELSINORE

• THE FIRST HONDA TO BE BUILT IN THE US •

THROUGHOUT THE 1960s, HONDA was devoted to producing models based on the four-stroke engine. However, as the '70s went by, it became obvious that to produce effective motocross machines it would need to develop two-stroke engines – the CR range of motocross bikes was the result. The popularity of motocross in the United States meant that when Honda built its first factory in Ohio, Elsinores were the first Hondas to come off the production line. The Elsinore model is named after a famous American motocross circuit.

Braced handlebars

Aluminum wheel with magnesium front and rear brake hubs

Lightweight drum brake

Metal footrest

Leading axle fork

BACK VIEW

SIDE VIEW

SPECIFICATIONS

- **ENGINE** Two-stroke, single cylinder
- **CAPACITY** 247cc
- **POWER OUTPUT** 40bhp
- **TRANSMISSION** Five-speed
- **WEIGHT** 224lb (102kg)
- **TOP SPEED** Not known

Fuel filler-cap

Plastic fuel tank reduces weight

Remote-reservoir shock absorber

Race numberplate

Plastic mudguard

HONDA

ELSINORE

Exhaust tailpipe

Radial fins help cool engine

Exhaust expansion chamber

18-in (46-cm) rear wheel has massive 5-in (13-cm) section rear tire

1983 CX650
• TURBOCHARGING FOR EXTRA POWER •

In the early 1980s, MOTORCYCLE manufacturers experimented with turbocharging. While other Japanese manufacturers took the logical step of basing their turbos on four-cylinder models, Honda's CX500 turbo, introduced in 1981, was based on the shaft-drive ohv V-twin CX500. The CX500 turbo was a testament to the ingenuity of the Honda research and development department, but the bike wasn't a sales success. Increasing the capacity to 673cc in 1983 resulted in the CX650 Turbo.

Passenger grab rail

Plastic side panel

Fuel injectors

"Pro-link" rear suspension linkage

Composite alloy wheel

SIDE VIEW

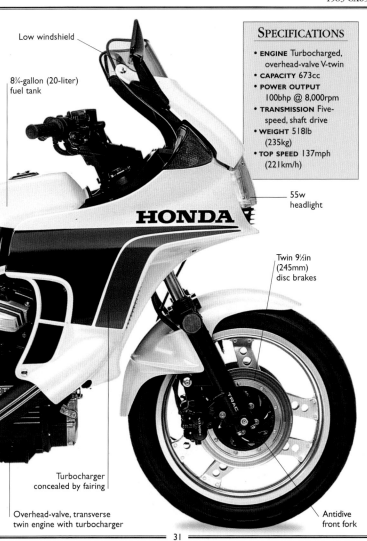

Low windshield

8¾-gallon (20-liter) fuel tank

SPECIFICATIONS

- **ENGINE** Turbocharged, overhead-valve V-twin
- **CAPACITY** 673cc
- **POWER OUTPUT** 100bhp @ 8,000rpm
- **TRANSMISSION** Five-speed, shaft drive
- **WEIGHT** 518lb (235kg)
- **TOP SPEED** 137mph (221km/h)

HONDA

55w headlight

Twin 9½in (245mm) disc brakes

Turbocharger concealed by fairing

Overhead-valve, transverse twin engine with turbocharger

Antidive front fork

1985 VF750F

• A NEW DIRECTION FOR HONDA'S SUPERBIKES •

HONDA WAS RESPONSIBLE FOR CREATING the classic in-line four-cylinder superbike layout which, by the early 1980s, was used by all the Japanese manufacturers. Honda sought to regain the competitive edge by adopting the "vee-four" engine layout in 1982. First available as a 750, the layout was soon used on a range of bikes from 400 to 1000cc. The compact design of the "vee-four" offered potential advantages, but it was initially problematic and expensive to produce. It never achieved the popularity that Honda expected, and the company soon reverted to the in-line four on all but its specialized sports bikes. This 1985 VF750 has been prepared for superbike racing and was ridden to victory in the Daytona 200 race.

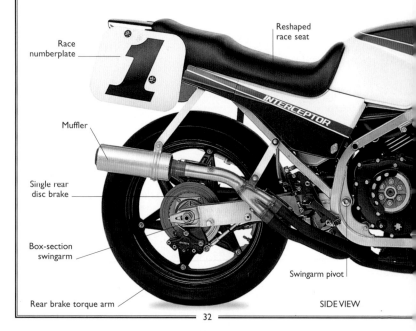

Race numberplate

Reshaped race seat

INTERCEPTOR

Muffler

Single rear disc brake

Box-section swingarm

Swingarm pivot

Rear brake torque arm

SIDE VIEW

INSIDE STORY

The Honda VF750 had a single suspension unit directly under the seat. The bike used square-section steel tubing, which has no great engineering merit and has since fallen out of favor among motorcycle manufacturers.

Braced headstock

BARE CHASSIS

Rear subframe supports seat and shock-absorber mounting

Quick-release fuel filler

Frame-mounted fairing

SPECIFICATIONS

- **ENGINE** 16-valve, double overhead cam, four-cylinder
- **CAPACITY** 748cc
- **POWER OUTPUT** 90bhp @ 10,000rpm
- **TRANSMISSION** Five-speed
- **WEIGHT** 510lb (231kg)
- **TOP SPEED** 132mph (213km/h) (Production model figures)

Lightweight mudguard

Twin front disc brakes

Box-section tubing

"Slick" race tire

1990 XRV750
• A DESERT-BEATING POWERHOUSE •

A NEW TYPE OF OFF-ROAD ENDURANCE marathon began in 1979 with the first Paris-Dakar Rally. The popularity of these events in Europe led to the creation of a large market for similar production machines. In 1989, Honda introduced its XRV750 "Africa Twin," which competed in the 1991 rally. It is based on the production bike but has increased fuel capacity and other adjustments to improve its rally performance.

Computerized compass mounted in slot behind seat

Additional fuel tank

Special desert tire

Modified exhaust system

Plastic shield protects rear disc

Toolbox

Navigation notes contained in "road book"

SPECIFICATIONS

- **ENGINE** Four-stroke, 52° V-twin
- **CAPACITY** 742cc
- **POWER OUTPUT** 59bhp @ 5,500rpm
- **TRANSMISSION** Five-speed, chain drive
- **WEIGHT** 463lb (210kg)
- **TOP SPEED** 115mph (185km/h)

(Production model figures)

Air intake positioned to stop sand getting in

BACK VIEW

Long-travel suspension

Fork protection shroud

Single disc brake

Water tank

Bashplate protects bottom of engine

SIDE VIEW

Tire filled with puncture-resistant mousse

1991 GL1500/6
• THE ULTIMATE IN TWO-WHEELED LUXURY •

THE ORIGINAL GOLDWING (see pp. 24–25) achieved real success only after it was fitted with a fairing and luggage panniers to create the ultimate in luxury tourers. The capacity of the original four-cylinder machine was increased to 1200cc before it was replaced by this gigantic 1520cc six-cylinder machine in 1988. This Wurlitzer on wheels features a mass of gizmos and gadgets, including a radio/cassette player, cruise control, and linked brakes. Most owners also add extra lights and more chrome trim. Rear suspension is by air spring, which can be adjusted from the saddle using an on-board compressor. The GL1500 is built at Honda's factory in the United States.

Passenger backrest

Storage pocket

Top box has removable luggage bag

Helmet lock

Pannier

Fold-down pannier side

Bike fitted with cast alloy wheels as standard

BACK VIEW

SIDE VIEW

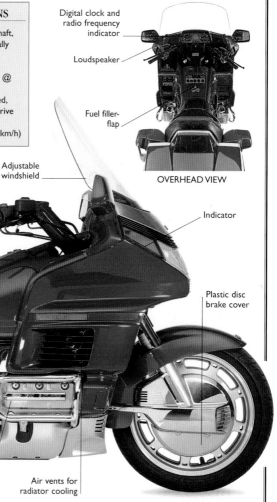

SPECIFICATIONS

- **ENGINE** Overhead camshaft, water-cooled, horizontally opposed, flat six
- **CAPACITY** 1520cc
- **POWER OUTPUT** 100bhp @ 5,200rpm
- **TRANSMISSION** Five-speed, electric reverse, shaft drive
- **WEIGHT** 811lb (368kg)
- **TOP SPEED** 116mph (187km/h)

Digital clock and radio frequency indicator

Loudspeaker

Fuel filler-flap

OVERHEAD VIEW

Adjustable windshield

Handlebar lever operates one front brake

Indicator

Radio-cassette player

Plastic disc brake cover

Flat six water-cooled engine

Air vents for radiator cooling

1993 CBR600F

• HONDA SETS THE STANDARD •

THE CBR600F HAS BEEN THE BENCHMARK middleweight sports bike ever since its introduction in 1987. For starters, the use of all-enclosed body panels was an innovative feature that allowed the engine to be built without aesthetic considerations. Conservative engineering – the CBR has an in-line four-cylinder engine and a steel frame – combined with Honda's traditional build quality has made the CBR600 a success. The design was heavily updated in 1991 to keep it ahead of the competition.

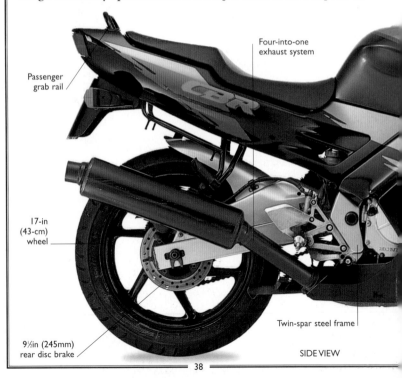

Four-into-one exhaust system

Passenger grab rail

17-in (43-cm) wheel

9½in (245mm) rear disc brake

Twin-spar steel frame

SIDE VIEW

SPECIFICATIONS

- **ENGINE** 16-valve, double overhead camshaft, in-line, four-cylinder
- **CAPACITY** 599cc
- **POWER OUTPUT** 99bhp @ 12,000rpm
- **TRANSMISSION** Six-speed
- **WEIGHT** 408lb (185kg)
- **TOP SPEED** 153mph (246km/h)

7-gallon (16-liter) fuel tank

Fork slider

Air duct

FRONT VIEW

HONDA

DIRECT INTAKE COOLING

600F

Four-piston brake calipers

Twin-disc front brake

Under the body panels hides a water-cooled, 16-valve, double overhead cam, four-cylinder engine

Alloy wheel

1997 CBR1100 BLACKBIRD

• THE FASTEST PRODUCTION BIKE AVAILABLE •

MOTORCYCLE MAKERS HAVE ALWAYS wanted to make the fastest bike on the market. Kawasaki claimed the title in 1990 with its ZZR1100, and it wasn't until six years later that Honda was able to respond. Placing a 164bhp engine in an aerodynamic bike weighing 531lb (241kg) resulted in a top speed of 177mph (285km/h). However, the Blackbird is also docile, easy to ride at low speed, comfortable, and has surprisingly agile handling. It combines the punch of a boxer with the manners of an English butler.

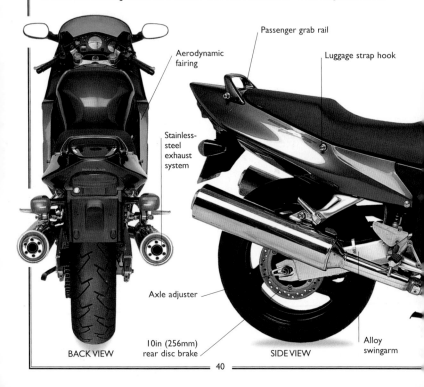

Passenger grab rail

Aerodynamic fairing

Luggage strap hook

Stainless-steel exhaust system

Axle adjuster

10in (256mm) rear disc brake

BACK VIEW

SIDE VIEW

Alloy swingarm

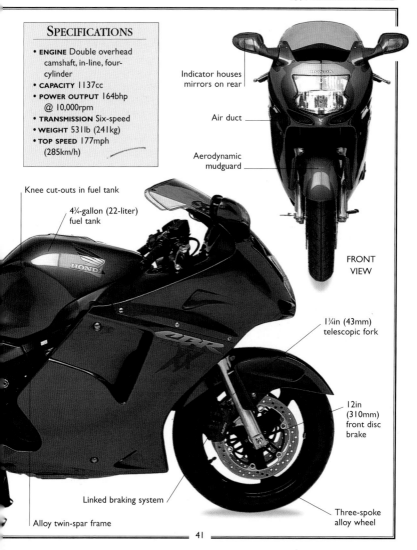

SPECIFICATIONS

- **ENGINE** Double overhead camshaft, in-line, four-cylinder
- **CAPACITY** 1137cc
- **POWER OUTPUT** 164bhp @ 10,000rpm
- **TRANSMISSION** Six-speed
- **WEIGHT** 531lb (241kg)
- **TOP SPEED** 177mph (285km/h)

Indicator houses mirrors on rear

Air duct

Aerodynamic mudguard

FRONT VIEW

Knee cut-outs in fuel tank

4¾-gallon (22-liter) fuel tank

1¾in (43mm) telescopic fork

12in (310mm) front disc brake

Linked braking system

Alloy twin-spar frame

Three-spoke alloy wheel

1997 VTR FIRESTORM

• SUPERBIKE SUCCESS IN THE 1990s •

FROM THE LATE 1960s, Honda was committed to developing impressive
four-cylinder superbikes. However, by the 1990s Ducati had achieved
success, winning sales, acclaim, and races with its good-looking, idiosyncratic
V-twin machines. Inspired by the Italian opposition, Honda soon built its
own V-twin. The Firestorm was a capable and, for Honda, quirky bike that
found a ready market among buyers who wanted the handling and power
of a lightweight V-twin without the suspect reliability of Italian machines.

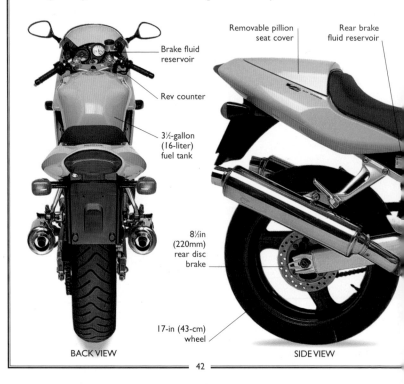

Brake fluid
reservoir

Rev counter

3½-gallon
(16-liter)
fuel tank

Removable pillion
seat cover

Rear brake
fluid reservoir

8½in
(220mm)
rear disc
brake

17-in (43-cm)
wheel

BACK VIEW

SIDE VIEW

Air duct

1½in (41mm)
telescopic fork

**FRONT
VIEW**

SPECIFICATIONS

- **ENGINE** Eight-valve, 90° V-twin
- **CAPACITY** 996cc
- **POWER OUTPUT** 108bhp
  @ 9,000rpm
- **TRANSMISSION** Six-speed
- **WEIGHT** 423lb (192kg)
- **TOP SPEED** 150mph (241km/h)

Aerodynamic
fairing

Alloy trellis
frame

Radiator

Adjustable
span brake
lever

11½in (296mm)
front disc brake

Clutch
cover

Swingarm pivot

Four-piston Nissin
brake calipers

Rear suspension linkage

INDEX

ACKNOWLEDGMENTS

AUTHOR'S ACKNOWLEDGMENTS:
Thanks to Phil Hunt and Mark Johnson-Davies
and to Louise Candlish, Tracy Hambleton-Miles,
and everyone else at DK. Thanks also to Dave
Dew, Scott Grimsdall, and Roger Harvey at
Honda (UK) (and my XR250 is brilliant). This
book is dedicated to Fred and Alex plus one.

**DORLING KINDERSLEY WOULD LIKE TO THANK
THE FOLLOWING FOR THEIR ASSISTANCE:**
Deutsches Zweirad Museum NSU Museum,
Neckarsulm, Germany; Motorcycle Heritage
Foundation, Westerville, Ohio; Honda of America;
Scott at Honda (UK); Mark Mederski; The
National Motor Museum, Beaulieu, UK; and The
National Motorcycle Museum, Birmingham, UK.

**DORLING KINDERSLEY WOULD LIKE TO THANK
THE FOLLOWING FOR THEIR KIND PERMISSION
TO USE THEIR PHOTOGRAPHS:**

Classic Bike/EMAP: 21 right.
Honda (UK): 15 top right.

All photography by Dave King and Andy Crawford.

NOTE
Every effort has been made to trace the copyright
holders. Dorling Kindersley apologizes for any
unintentional omissions and would be pleased,
in such cases, to add an acknowledgment in
future editions.